MAGICAL
SEASCAPES
COLORING BOOK

Miryam Adatto

Dover Publications, Inc.
Mineola, New York

Aug 2018

Imagine a fantastic sea landscape complete with swirling waves, stunning underwater flora and fauna, perhaps a sunrise or a lighthouse—much like the beautifully detailed images you'll find in this collection. Sixty-three black-and-white drawings, intended for the advanced colorist, provide the canvas for you to bring the scenes alive with color to create your very own magical seascapes. Plus, the pages are perforated and printed on one side only, so you can easily display your finished artwork.

Bibliographical Note

Magical SeaScapes Coloring Book is a new work, first published
by Dover Publications, Inc., in 2017.

International Standard Book Number

ISBN-13: 978-0-486-81854-2
ISBN-10: 0-486-81854-3

Manufactured in the United States by LSC Communications
81854301   2017
www.doverpublications.com